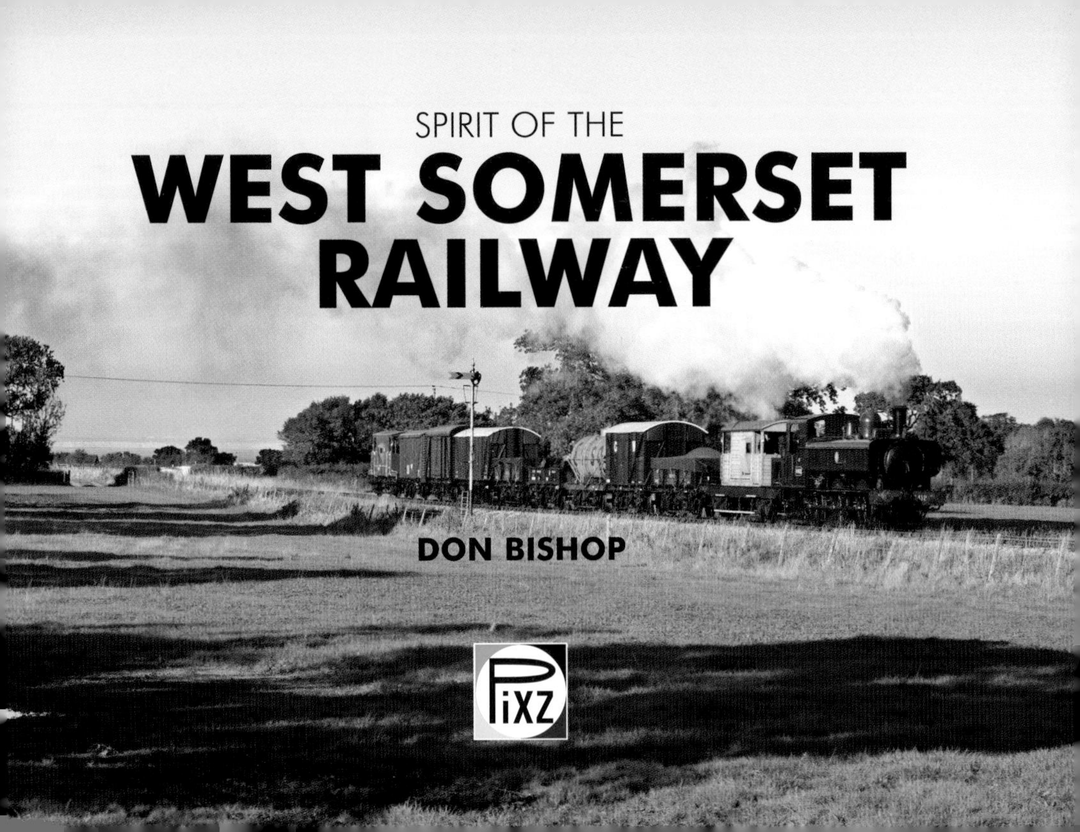

SPIRIT OF THE

WEST SOMERSET RAILWAY

DON BISHOP

PiXZ

First published in Great Britain in 2009

British Library Cataloguing-in-Publication Data
A CIP record for this title is available from the British Library

ISBN 978 1 906887 26 1

PiXZ Books
Halsgrove House, Ryelands Industrial Estate, Bagley Road,
Wellington, Somerset TA21 9PZ
Tel: 01823 653777
Fax: 01823 216796
email: sales@halsgrove.com

An imprint of Halstar Ltd, part of the Halsgrove group of companies
Information on all Halsgrove ttles is available at: www.halsgrove.com

Printed and bound by Grafiche Flaminia, Italy

Introduction

In this pocket-sized book, a second volume of his work on the very popular West Somerset Railway, Don Bishop has put together a selection of 60 images of the line taken over the last few years showing the variety of steam locomotives that have run on the 23 mile line between Bishops Lydeard, near Taunton, and Minehead.

The line runs through the Quantock Hills, an Area of Outstanding Natural Beauty, from Bishops Lydeard climbing 4 miles to the summit of the line at Crowcombe Heathfield before continuing back downhill through Stogumber and Williton to the coast at Watchet. After a stop here the 1874 extension of the line to Minehead commences by climbing inland to the village of Washford before turning back to the coast again at Blue Anchor. It then follows the coast close by through the edge of Dunster to the terminus on the seafront at Minehead, a full 20 miles from Bishops Lydeard making the line the longest standard gauge heritage line in the UK.

There is also a further 3 mile section of track between Bishops Lydeard and Norton Fitzwarren Junction, where the line joins the mainline network. At Norton Fitzwarren the West Somerset Railway Association is busy building a turning triangle on 38 acres of land they purchased in 2006, and longer term possible further developments, to enhance the railway's ability to provide facilities to turn locomotives and trains coming onto the WSR from the mainline. This will be in addition to the newly commissioned turntable at Minehead, which was brought into use during 2008.

This small volume portrays the line at its scenic best out in the lovely countryside that surrounds it. Most of the shots were taken in the cooler months of the year between October and April when steam photography is much better. It therefore also includes the line's annual Spring, Autumn and Winter Gala events which are very popular with enthusiasts and the general public alike for putting on an exceptional show of steam power.

Don Bishop ARPS
West Huntspill

S&D 7F 2-8-0 No. 88 pilots Black 5 No. 45231 past Kentsford near Watchet with a through excursion from London to Minehead on 30th September 2006.

The 7F passes Watersmeet near Bishops Lydeard a little while after sunset with a Santa Special working on 27th November 2005.

Opposite page: During the line's 2006 Somerset & Dorset Gala the resident S&D 7F No. 88 pilots BR Standard 5 No. 73129 past Nethercott with a Minehead-bound train of maroon stock. 19th March 2006.

A dramatic departure from Bishops Lydeard in wonderful low light conditions, only possible in December, as 7F No. 88 takes a train of children to see Santa on 17th December 2006.

Terrier No. 662 Martello paid a visit to the line in late 2007 and is seen leaving Minehead with a shuttle bound for Blue Anchor on 29th December 2007.

A night scene at Minehead shed on 27th October 2007 sees No. 62 Martello resting after its day's work on the line between Minehead, Dunster and Blue Anchor.

Opposite page: GWR 0-4-2T No. 1450 heads a two coach auto train past Nornvis Bridge near Crowcombe on 4th October 2007.

G W R

Mike Little's 14xx Auto tank No. 1450 heads his matching auto coach No. 178 past Liddymore between Watchet and Williton on 15th March 2005.

Record-breaking GWR 4-4-0 No. 3440 City of Truro pilots 0-6-2T No. 6619 from the North Yorkshire Moors Railway past vintage road vehicles at Roebuck Crossing on 7th October 2007.

Reputedly the first 100 mph locomotive in the world (in 1904), GWR City 4-4-0 No. 3440 City of Truro passes Water Lane near Stogumber with a Bishops Lydeard-bound train on 4th October 2007.

Opposite page: Llangollen Railway based GW 38xx 2-8-0 No. 3802 climbing the bank out of Watchet at Kentsford Farm on 5th October 2007.

G W R

38xx 2-8-0 No. 3850 passing Combe Florey with a winter service to Minehead on 29th December 2007.

Opposite page: A rather overgrown scene at Nethercott on 4th October 2007 sees No. 3850 passing with a Minehead-bound service.

GW 2-8-0 No. 3850 passing Watersmeet with a Bishops Lydeard – Williton Santa Express on 7th December 2008.

Opposite page: WSR-based large Prairie No. 4160 pilots Castle No. 5051 Earl Bathurst from Didcot, at Eastcombe near Bishops Lydeard, with a photo charter on 16th March 2007.

Large Prairie No. 4160 arrives at Blue Anchor on 18th May 2008 with a Bishops Lydeard-bound train. The 'lean' of the signal on the left is caused by the use of a wide angle lens and does not actually lean as it appears in reality!

Opposite page: With the Bristol channel in the background No. 4160 gets away from Williton with a Bishops Lydeard-bound train on 27th March 2008.

A warm spring made things 'green up' rather quickly in 2007,
No. 4160 enters the curve at Roebuck on 29th May 2007.

Opposite page: Didcot's Castle No. 5051 Earl Bathurst was repainted into BR green livery at the request of the author in 2007 and is seen climbing the grade at Nethercott in its new livery with the Quantock Hills behind on 17th March 2007.

Langollen based large Prairie No. 5199 and Hall No. 4936 Kinlet Hall are illuminated by weak sunshine as they round the curve at Doniford with a Minehead-bound train 1st October 2004.

Opposite page: On a photo charter No. 5199 is worked downhill at Sampford Brett with a goods train on 4th October 2004.

5199
1326

Rather dull conditions prevail at Combe Florey as Pete Waterman's GW 2-8-0T No. 5224 heads a goods working towards Minehead on 13th March 2008.

Opposite page: Bill Parker's newly restored small Prairie No. 5521 arrives at Blue Anchor on 11th March 2007. This has to date been the engine's only UK heritage line visit as soon after this it went over to Poland and Hungary for a spell, and was still over in mainland Europe in Jan 2009 when this book was prepared.

GREAT WESTERN
COLMANS
MUSTARD

5542
G W R
5542

At a location intriguingly known as Turks Castle No. 5542 climbs uphill towards Stogumber on 6th March 2005.

Opposite page: Small Prairies Nos. 5542 and 5553 passing Liddymore with a Minehead to Bishops Lydeard train on 9th March 2008.

Bodmin Railway-based small Prairie No. 5552 is seen at Sampford Brett. 23rd March 2004.

Opposite page:
The same photo charter as in the above image, passing Castle Hill near Williton with a goods train on 23rd March 2004.

Pete Waterman's small Prairie No. 5553 has spent most of its preservation career on the WSR to date. On 2nd October 2005 it heads the Quantock Belle dining train set and other stock past Bicknoller.

Prairie No. 5553 picks up the early morning light as it passes Cotford sidings at Bishops Lydeard with a photo charter running on the Norton Fitzwarren to Bishops Lydeard section on the morning of 2nd January 2004.

WSR based small Prairie No. 5553 passes through Doniford Halt with a Bishops Lydeard-bound service on 30th October 2005.

Opposite page:
No. 5553 passes the caravan site at Helwell Bay, Watchet on 3rd March 2007.

5553

5553

The ever popular small Prairie No. 5553 passing Yarde Farm with the 10.15 Minehead to Bishops Lydeard service on 29th April 2006.

Opposite page: The Quantock Belle leaves Blue Anchor behind – No. 5553 in the last of the day's sunlight on 6th March 2005.

King No. 6024 King Edward 1 approaching Washford at Bye Farm with a Minehead-bound service during the Spring Gala on 20th March 2005.

Opposite page: WSRA-owned Pannier No. 6412 climbing Washford Bank at Horse Parks with a driver experience goods working on 4th November 2006. The engine was sold to the South Devon Railway at the end of 2008.

6412

Severn Valley Railway-based Manor 4-6-0 No. 7802 Bradley Manor at Bye Farm on the climb from Watchet to Washford on 18th March 2007.

Opposite page: Pannier No. 6412 climbs the final stretch of 1 in 65 into Washford Station with a Bishops Lydeard-bound service on 3rd March 2007.

A classic Manor and Castle combination of No. 7822 Foxcote Manor and 5051 Earl Bathurst working hard past Kentsford with a photo charter working on 13th March 2007.

Opposite page: A real mainline feel is captured at Bicknoller as Manor No. 7822 Foxcote Manor and Castle No. 5051 Earl Bathurst work downhill at Bicknoller with a photo charter on 13th March 2007.

Earlier the same day 7822 Foxcote Manor and 5051 Earl Bathurst create further scenes reminiscent of the South Devon Banks at Nethercott with the photo charter.

Steam in the Quantock Hills – WSR Mogul No. 9351 and Prairie No. 5199 climbing past Nethercott, West Somerset Railway with a Minehead-bound train on 30th September 2004.

G W R
935

A Santa Express working to Williton sets out from Bishops Lydeard at Whisky Trail on 11th December 2005 behind No. 9351 – affectionately known among WSR staff as the Mongrel.

Opposite page: WSR-designed small GW Mogul No. 9351 passing Nornvis on the approach to Crowcombe with a Bishops Lydeard to Minehead train on 28th December 2004.

West Country Pacific No. 34007 Wadebridge working past the site of Leigh Bridge loop between Stogumber and Crowcombe in soft afternoon lighting on 28th March 2007.

Opposite page: BR Black Terrier No. 32678 recreates something of the Southern Region branch line scene as it crosses Ker Moor between Blue Anchor and Dunster on 30th September 2004.

West Country No. 34046 Braunton at Bishops Lydeard during its official launch with engineers Gareth Winter (Project Leader) and Keith Speller. 24th September 2008.

Opposite page: West Country No. 34046 Braunton is turned on Minehead's new turntable in the pouring rain on 5th October 2008.

34046
BRAUNTON
12

Merchant Navy Pacific No. 35005 Canadian Pacific from the Mid Hants Railway paid a visit to the WSR for the Autumn 2005 Gala. Here it passes Kentsford near Watchet with an afternoon train to Minehead on 2nd October 2005.

Stanier Mogul No. 42968 leaving Crowcombe Heathfield Station in rather dull lighting conditions with a Minehead-bound service on 6th October 2007. The engine is normally based on the Severn Valley Railway.

A classic Somerset & Dorset scene, and some may say typical Mendip weather too! Midland 4F No. 44422 pilots Southern Pacific No. 34067 Tangmere away from Bishops Lydeard on 20th March 2006.

Opposite page: Midland region duo 4F No. 44422 and Stanier Mogul No. 42968 climb the 1 in 80 grade round the curve at Churchlands near Combe Florey with a Minehead-bound service on 4th October 2007. The coach colour has been modified digitally.

In a brief spell of sunshine LNWR Super D No. 49395 passes Bicknoller with a Bishops Lydeard-bound gala service on 15th March 2008.

Opposite page: At the same location, but in rather cleaner condition – not typical of the class in steam days, the Super D passes Bicknoller on 2nd October 2005.

Another classic Somerset & Dorset combination, S&D 7F No. 53809 and Bulleid 'Battle of Britain' No. 34067 Tangmere leave Bishops Lydeard with a photo charter on a dull and dank 21st March 2006.

Opposite page: Perhaps one of the most unusual visitors to the WSR was Great Eastern J15 0-6-0 No. 65462, here passing Castle Hill near Williton on 22nd March 2004 with a photo charter goods train.

BRITISH RAILWAYS
65462

Great Eastern J15 0-6-0 No. 65462 is again seen with its charter goods on 22nd March 2004, this time in pleasant back lighting at Roebuck curve.

BR Standard 4 No. 76079 pilots Bulleid 'Battle of Britain' No. 34067 Tangmere through the hamlet of Nethercott on the climb to Crowcombe on 19th March 2006, during the hugely successful S&D Gala.

The Bristol Channel forms the backdrop to this shot of BR Standard tank No. 80136 rounding the curve on the cliff tops at Doniford on 1st May 2006.

Opposite page: Standard 2-6-4T No. 80136 passing a location known to WSR staff as Teddy Bear's Crossing near Williton with a photo charter on 16th April 2007.

Long-term WSR resident Standard tank No. 80136 passing Sampford Brett
and Woolston with a Bishops Lydeard-bound train on 31st December 2004.